G000127448

summersdale

BORED STUPID!

Summersdale Publishers Ltd
46 West Street
Chichester
West Sussex
PO19 1RP
UK

www.summersdale.com

Printed and bound in Great Britain

ISBN 1 84024 473 9

Invent a
dance move.

Polish a
lamp-post.

Floss a gate.

Wear safety specs at all times.

Plait your
hamster's hair.

Paint a tree pink.

Dig your own grave.

Learn the lyrics to all of Eminem's songs and shout them out your window at 5 a.m.

Make yourself
a king and
establish your
own kingdom.

Take up your bedroom carpet.

Put it back
— upside-down.

Replace political
campaign signs
with pictures
of pirates.

Open a stud
farm for
racing snails.

Paint yellow
polka-dots
on your
sister's car.

Call the Talking Clock and tell it your problems.

Remember.

Forget.

Create a website for your cat.

Kidnap a
cartoon
character.

Ask for
directions to
the corner
shop.

Find anagrams of your name.

Bring a
cupboard
to school.

Fill your dad's
shoes with
raspberry jam.

Repeat a word
over and over
until it loses
its meaning.

Wait for the apocalypse.

Go to a couple's counselling session with your teddy bear.

Read the
*Encyclopaedia
Britannica*
backwards.

BORED
Stupid!

Contemplate
a fork.

Live in a box.

BORED
Stupid!

Stare at
someone
until they turn
around.

33

Learn all you can about the history of green.

Watch all three
*Lord of the
Rings* films
in Chinese.

Play hide-
and-seek
with a shrub.

Play squash
blindfolded.

Make up a
language.

Memorise the phone book.

Don't do it.

Do it.

Repeat
everything
everyone says
in an Italian
accent.

Kiss a potato.

Pass go.

Ring a friend you haven't spoken to in years. Then tell them you're busy and you have to go.

45

Post a
mushroom
to the Prime
Minister.

Ring
McDonald's
and complain
about the food.

Write a book
about snow.

BORED Stupid!

Defend your right to wear a chicken on your head.

49

Grow wings.

BORED
Stupid!

Become a mime.

Campaign to
have cream
cheese named
the national
food.

Climb the
corporate
ladder.

Climb down again.

BORED
STUPID!

Ask for 1p
from everyone
and become
a millionaire.

55

Place a personal ad for your dog.

Put jelly in
your brother's
inflatable chair.

BORED
StuPid!

Alphabetise
your spice rack.

Stand outside.

Play football
with a
cauliflower.
Put a broccoli
in goal.

Don't fall over.

Promise to be good.

Crochet a jacket for your school desk.

Cry wolf.

Cook a book.

Donate apples
to your local
petshop.

BORED
Stupid!

Adopt a flea.

Bury your
pillow.

Bubble-wrap
your sofa.

Make an
audition tape
for a reality
TV show.

Create a
computer virus.

BORED **StUPid!**

Phone your favourite primary school teachers and tell them you're going to the toilet.

72

Whenever
anyone tells
you anything,
demand that
they prove it.

Discover a
new country.

Give your
staples names.

BORED
Stupid!

Enter your pet
turnip in the
London City
Marathon.

76

Ascend to a
higher plane
of existence.

Chase a flower.

BORED
Stupid!

Pretend to
be Scottish
for a day.

Guess what
food the people
at the next
table will order.

BORED
Stupid!

Massage a beanbag.

Look disgusted
when people
call your name.

Hold a press conference.

BORED
Stupid!

Time how
long it takes
for your skin
to go wrinkly
in the bath.

84

Listen to a sad song and laugh.

Gargle the
alphabet
backwards.

Buy a dream catcher and look for the trapped dreams in the morning.

Stroke walls
whenever
possible.

Look for the Magic Eye picture in carpet designs.

Search for your
identical twin.

BORED Stupid!

Yell 'Geronimo' whenever you go up- or downstairs.

91

Marry your fish.

Blame the cat.

Stack all the
books you own
into one pillar.

Invent a new colour.

List all the people you know.

Video a brick
and track its
progress.

Chase a fly.

Make posters explaining the meaning of life.

Turn up to
school in
fancy dress.

Create a
yawning
epidemic in a
crowded place.

Start a petition to ban wasps.

Hop on one foot.

Housetrain a woodlouse.

Watch the
moon and see
if it falls.

Wear all the
clothes you
own at the
same time.

Paint your face
like a tiger
without using
a mirror.

Draw an
ordnance
survey map of
your bedroom.

Get lost.

BORED
Stupid!

Stalk your
neighbour's
cat.

110

Tap dance
when crossing
the street.

Pick a fight
with a squirrel,
explaining
that whoever
runs away
first loses.

Go back three spaces.

Find out which
dries faster,
vinyl or gloss.

Remove all the DVDs from your dad's collection and put them back in the wrong boxes.

Find a hidden
meaning in
everything.

Write all
your letters
in alphabet
spaghetti.

Get on your nerves.

Plant an umbrella.

Count.

Write a love
story involving
your favourite
Lego figures.
Submit it to
Mills and Boon.

Sail the seven seas.

Speak in riddles.

Wrestle a chair.

BORED
Stupid!

Rewrite the
rules of chess.

Give a radiator a makeover.

Teach yourself telepathy.

Make a list of
things to do
when bored.